Coast Guard: Enforcement Under MARPOL V Convention on Pollution Expanded, Although Problems Remain

United States Government Accountability Office Resources, Community, and Economic Development Division

United States General Accounting Office

GAO

Report to Congressional Requesters

May 1995

COAST GUARD

Enforcement Under MARPOL V Convention on Pollution Expanded, Although Problems Remain

GAO/RCED-95-143

United States
General Accounting Office
Washington, D.C. 20548

Resources, Community, and
Economic Development Division

B-260210

letter date goes here

The Honorable Mark O. Hatfield
Chairman, Committee on Appropriations
United States Senate

The Honorable Frank R. Lautenberg
Ranking Minority Member
Subcommittee on Transportation
Committee on Appropriations
United States Senate

As much as 1 million metric tons of garbage and plastics enter the ocean each year, killing seabirds and marine mammals, creating safety hazards for shippers and boaters, and polluting shorelines and beaches. To mitigate the uncontrolled ocean dumping of garbage and plastics, the United States became a party to annex V of the International Convention for the Prevention of Pollution From Ships (known as MARPOL V), which placed restrictions on the discharge of garbage and plastics from ships of signatory countries. The Congress ratified, and the President signed into law, the provisions of MARPOL V as part of the Marine Plastic Pollution Research and Control Act of 1987. The act charged the Secretary of Transportation, who delegated his responsibility to the U.S. Coast Guard, with enforcing MARPOL V.

Since the passage of the act, the Congress has repeatedly expressed concerns about the Coast Guard's enforcement efforts.[1] To enhance MARPOL enforcement, the Senate Committee on Appropriations provided for 100 MARPOL enforcement positions beginning in fiscal year 1991.[2] As part of the Senate report that accompanied the Department of Transportation's 1994 appropriations bill, the Committee requested that we provide information on the Coast Guard's enforcement of MARPOL V. Specifically, our report discusses what progress the Coast Guard has made in its effort to enforce MARPOL V and whether the positions the Congress funded are being utilized for MARPOL-related purposes. In addition, the

---

[1]Senate Report on the Department of Transportation and Related Agencies Appropriation Bill, 1991, Report 101-398 (July 27, 1990); and Implementation of the Marine Plastic Pollution Research and Control Act, Hearing before the Subcommittee on Superfund, Ocean, and Water Protection, Senate Committee on Environment and Public Works (Sept. 17, 1992).

[2]The report by the Senate Committee on Appropriations provided that pollution prevention investigation positions be used for the enforcement of MARPOL (including annexes I, II, and V), the Shore Protection Act, and the Ocean Dumping Ban Act.

GAO/RCED-95-143 Enforcement Under MARPOL V

report describes the Coast Guard's educational and outreach efforts, which are also intended to improve compliance with MARPOL V.

Results in Brief

Although the provisions of MARPOL V became effective on December 31, 1988, the Coast Guard did not begin substantial enforcement efforts until the early 1990s. Following congressional criticism in 1990 and 1992, and aided by additional personnel, the Coast Guard stepped up its enforcement efforts. The number of reported cases involving violations of the MARPOL V regulations has increased steadily from 16 in 1989 to 311 in 1994. Fewer than 10 percent of all cases have resulted in any penalties being assessed on the violator, although a significant number are still being processed.

At present, no accurate means exists to determine whether the Coast Guard is fully utilizing the additional resources that the Congress provided for enforcing MARPOL. While nearly all of the designated enforcement positions are filled, the people who occupy them also perform many other activities unrelated to MARPOL. In addition to the designated enforcement positions, the Coast Guard spreads its efforts to enforce MARPOL across many field personnel. However, just how much time the Coast Guard, in aggregate, spends on MARPOL-related activities is uncertain because the Coast Guard does not consistently record time spent on this function.

Education and outreach has become an important part of the Coast Guard's strategy to achieve compliance with MARPOL. In 1994, the Coast Guard's education and outreach efforts for MARPOL V expanded from targeting commercial shippers to include other groups, such as recreational boaters and fishing vessel operators. Through a program called SeaPartners, which has been funded by nearly $3 million in grants from the Department of Defense, the Coast Guard has conducted more than a thousand community-based activities for boating groups, port operators, students, and others. A recent Coast Guard-commissioned evaluation of SeaPartners found that these activities needed to be better focused. In response, the Coast Guard is now revising its SeaPartners strategy.

Background

The Marine Plastic Pollution Research and Control Act of 1987 incorporates the provisions of MARPOL V that make it illegal for U.S. or foreign ships to discharge any plastics, including synthetic ropes, fishing nets, and plastic bags, into the ocean and other navigable waters. In 1989, the Coast Guard first promulgated regulations to enforce the MARPOL V provisions.[3] These regulations specify that other forms of garbage, such as food waste and packing materials, may not be discharged within prescribed limits of U.S. shorelines.[4] For U.S.-licensed boats above a certain size, the regulations require operators to post garbage discharge warning signs, maintain an approved waste management plan, and keep records of garbage disposal and discharges. For all vessels, U.S. and foreign, the regulations also set out the MARPOL V provisions against the illegal discharge of plastic and garbage, as well as the Coast Guard's inspection procedures and possible penalties for infractions.

The Coast Guard enforces compliance with MARPOL V mainly through its regional network of 47 marine safety offices.[5] Enforcement personnel regularly inspect foreign and U.S.-licensed vessels for compliance with various safety and pollution regulations, including MARPOL V. If enforcement personnel find a violation of MARPOL V during their inspections, they document their findings and open an enforcement case on the Coast Guard's computer system, the marine safety information system. The case is then forwarded to the district office, which reviews it for completeness and the sufficiency of evidence. If the district office finds the evidence to be sufficient, it forwards the case to one of three Coast Guard hearing offices for a civil penalty determination.[6]

In addition to the Coast Guard's inspections, inspectors from the U.S. Department of Agriculture's Animal and Plant Health Inspection Service (APHIS) also inspect commercial ships. APHIS inspects a majority of ships arriving from foreign ports, typically within 24 hours of their arrival, for compliance with U.S. plant and animal health laws. While APHIS is not required by law to enforce MARPOL V, it agreed in 1990 to help the Coast Guard do so. If APHIS suspects that a violation of MARPOL V has occurred, APHIS inspectors are supposed to notify the local Coast Guard marine safety office.

---

[3]Implementing regulations are found in the Code of Federal Regulations (33 C.F.R. 151, sections 51 through 77). The regulations have been amended four times since 1989 (see footnote 7).

[4]Under the MARPOL V regulations, it is illegal to dump plastics or garbage in U.S. lakes and rivers and within 3 miles of ocean shorelines. Garbage ground to less than 1 inch square can be disposed of more than 3 miles from shore (in the ocean); regulations do not permit the disposal of plastics.

[5]Other Coast Guard field personnel—such as those assigned to small boat and air stations—are also responsible for the enforcement of MARPOL V in conjunction with their other responsibilities.

[6]In 1978, the Coast Guard established a civil penalty hearing procedure whereby cases are decided by Coast Guard hearing officers who are independent of the command structure. Suspected criminal violations are referred to the U.S. Attorney's office. Violations by foreign-flagged vessels that occur outside the U.S. 200-mile Exclusive Economic Zone are referred to the country where the vessel is registered.

Coast Guard Enforcement Has Increased, but Problems Remain

The Coast Guard intensified its enforcement of MARPOL V following congressional criticism in 1990 and 1992 of the Coast Guard's lack of progress in implementing MARPOL V. More aggressive enforcement, according to Coast Guard officials, has resulted in a steady increase in the number of MARPOL V violations found by enforcement personnel. Even so, the Coast Guard's enforcement efforts have been affected by factors that affect the ability of its enforcement personnel to identify violations and adequately support their findings so that violators are penalized.

Number of MARPOL V Enforcement Cases Has Increased

The Coast Guard has identified an increasing number of violations of the MARPOL V regulations in recent years. In the first few years of the program, unless a violation was egregious, Coast Guard officials in the field said they often allowed violators to correct any problems and did not take enforcement actions. Since 1992, however, following increased congressional attention and aided by additional resources, the Coast Guard has strengthened the MARPOL V regulations and emphasized the need for personnel to be more aggressive in their enforcement.[7] Accordingly, the number of enforcement cases involving violations of MARPOL V has increased from 16 in 1989, the first year of implementation, to 311 during 1994 (see fig. 1 and app. I for additional analysis of these violations).[8]

---

[7]Since 1989, when the Coast Guard issued interim MARPOL V regulations, it has strengthened the regulations or their interpretation on four occasions. In 1990, the Coast Guard required that an approved waste management plan be aboard U.S.-licensed ships over 40 feet. In 1991, it required U.S.-licensed ships more than 26 feet in length to post signs listing garbage discharge restrictions. In 1992, the Coast Guard expanded its jurisdiction over foreign-licensed vessels from 3 miles to 200 mile off U.S. shores. In 1994, the Coast Guard required U.S. commercial vessels over 40 feet in length to keep refuse discharge records.

[8]These data are drawn from the Office of Marine Safety's marine safety information computer system According to Coast Guard officials in other offices, the Coast Guard does not collect complete MARPOL V enforcement data from offices other than marine safety offices—for example, data on possible violations found by small boat station personnel.

Figure 1: Coast Guard's MARPOL V Enforcement Cases, 1989-94

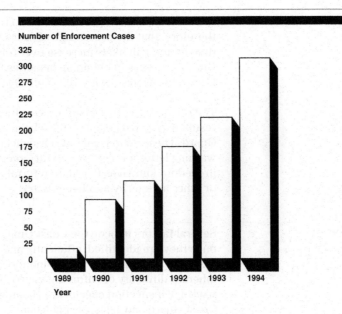

Number of Enforcement Cases

Source: The Coast Guard's marine safety information system.

An increasing number of marine safety offices have initiated MARPOL V enforcement cases, indicating that the Coast Guard's enforcement efforts are becoming more widespread. During 1991, two marine safety offices (New York and Corpus Christi) accounted for more than half of all enforcement cases, and only 20 of the 47 marine safety offices had initiated any cases. By 1994, the distribution of cases had become less concentrated—the five marine safety offices with the most cases accounted for more than half of all enforcement cases. Also, 33 marine safety offices had initiated at least one MARPOL V enforcement case.

Few Enforcement Cases Have Resulted in Penalties

Of the 725 MARPOL V cases reported as of February 15, 1995, 69, or just under 10 percent, have resulted in the assessment of a penalty against the responsible party.[9] The penalties ranged from a few hundred dollars to $50,000 and averaged almost $6,200 per case. However, 303, or 42 percent, of the cases submitted are still in process, including two-thirds of all the cases initiated in 1994. It is reasonable to assume that some percentage of

[9]For additional detail on the nature, status, and disposition of the 725 violations, see app. I.

the 303 cases still in process will also result in a penalty assessment and, therefore, that the percentage of cases which result in a penalty for this time period will likely increase over time.[10] However, whether the Coast Guard's success in obtaining penalties is improving over time is not yet known because so many 1993 and 1994 cases are still being processed.

The remaining enforcement cases—those not in process or not having resulted in a civil penalty—have been administratively settled by the Coast Guard. These actions include case closure or dismissal, the issuance of a warning letter, or a referral to the country where the ship is registered—a procedure known as flag state referral—for consideration of possible fines or other actions by another country.

Coast Guard's Enforcement Efforts Impeded by Several Factors

Several factors impede the Coast Guard's efforts to identify violations and, once they are identified, efficiently and effectively process enforcement cases for a civil penalty determination. Among these factors are (1) the inherent difficulty of enforcing MARPOL V, (2) the absence of a standardized MARPOL V inspection checklist, (3) diminished cooperation between the Coast Guard and APHIS, (4) inadequate feedback on case development, and (5) a burdensome and ineffective management information system.

Enforcing the MARPOL V Regulations on Garbage Discharge Is Inherently Difficult

To cite a vessel for illegally discharging garbage or plastics, someone must see the event and report it, or the Coast Guard must develop strong evidence that such a discharge occurred. It is rare that Coast Guard personnel or others actually witness a vessel illegally disposing of plastics or other garbage. A Coast Guard hearing officer told us that unlike oil or hazardous waste discharges, discharges of plastics and other garbage usually do not leave a trail of evidence that can be traced to the offending party. According to Coast Guard officials in the field, should vessel operators knowingly choose to violate the MARPOL V discharge regulations, it is unlikely that they will be caught.

Complicating enforcement efforts is the fact that one key component of the U.S. MARPOL V regulations—a requirement that vessels maintain garbage discharge records—does not apply to foreign-licensed ships.[11] This difference is significant because a garbage discharge record is one of

[10]For example, comparing the 69 cases that have resulted in a penalty against the 422 cases thus far completed yields a 16-percent penalty rate.

[11]The Coast Guard has actively sought to strengthen the MARPOL treaty within the International Maritime Organization. Members of this international body have agreed in principal to amend the MARPOL convention to require garbage discharge and other records similar to those now in force for U.S. vessels. Final adoption is expected shortly, according to Coast Guard headquarters officials.

the key items that the Coast Guard uses as evidence in enforcement cases to prove that an illegal discharge has occurred. Equally significant, the Coast Guard can enforce MARPOL V for foreign vessels only within the U.S. Exclusive Economic Zone.[12] Demonstrating that a vessel discharged garbage at sea is difficult; proving that it occurred within U.S. jurisdiction is even more difficult.

Enforcement Personnel Lack a Standardized MARPOL V Inspection Checklist

Because eyewitness accounts of illegal discharges are infrequent, the Coast Guard often must develop circumstantial evidence that would lead to a prima facie determination that a discharge violation had occurred. Proving that a violation has occurred on the basis of circumstantial evidence is not easy and requires Coast Guard personnel to conduct a thorough and methodical investigation while on board a vessel. This includes gathering statements, checking the ship's food storage and garbage disposal areas, taking photographs, and examining logbooks and other records.

To help personnel enforce a wide variety of safety and pollution regulations, the Coast Guard relies extensively on standardized inspection checklists. The Coast Guard recognizes the importance of these checklists in helping to identify violations and develop sufficient evidence to support an enforcement action. However, according to the Chief of the Marine Environmental Protection Division, a standardized checklist covering the MARPOL V portion of vessel inspections has not been developed because of competing priorities.

In our visits to marine inspection offices, we found a variety of boarding checklists. For the inspections of foreign vessels, each office had devised its own checklist, which ranged from lists with a single reference to MARPOL V to lists containing several pages of questions and guidance. For inspections of U.S. vessels and foreign passenger ships, the Coast Guard provides standardized inspection booklets to its inspectors. However, because these booklets predate MARPOL V, they do not include any reference to MARPOL V. In some offices, these booklets have been updated to remind inspectors to check on compliance with MARPOL V, but updates have not been standardized among marine safety offices.

The absence of a standard inspection checklist for MARPOL V can hinder the ability of enforcement personnel to identify violations and then develop sufficient evidence to support an enforcement action. During one inspection we witnessed, for example, the port safety officer used a

---

[12]The Exclusive Economic Zone generally extends 200 miles from U.S. shorelines.

checklist with only a single reference to MARPOL V and did not identify violations that his superior later acknowledged should have been cited. In other marine safety offices, where more extensive checklists were used, we saw more thorough examinations, involving extensive inspections of food storage, food preparation, and garbage disposal areas and a detailed questioning of the crew on garbage disposal practices. Coast Guard officials responsible for the MARPOL V program agreed that the inspection checklist should be standardized and, on the basis of our findings, told us that they will initiate steps to develop one.

Cooperation Between the Coast Guard and APHIS Could Improve MARPOL V Enforcement Efforts

The extent of cooperation between the Coast Guard and APHIS has varied in some locations. During the first years of MARPOL V enforcement, APHIS was an important source for identifying MARPOL V violations. Now, however, cutbacks in APHIS' funding and uncertainties about the extent of APHIS' role in MARPOL V inspections have diminished cooperation between the agencies in some locations.

On three separate occasions beginning in 1990, APHIS headquarters has directed its field units to cooperate with the Coast Guard in identifying MARPOL V violations. APHIS headquarters provided criteria for its field units to use as a basis for forwarding copies of their inspection reports to the appropriate Coast Guard marine safety office for possible action. During our visits to marine safety offices, we found instances of substantial cooperation between the two agencies that had resulted in numerous enforcement cases in recent years. For example, in one marine safety office, the two agencies had conducted joint training: APHIS had instructed the Coast Guard on how to identify Asian Gypsy Moths, and the Coast Guard had provided MARPOL V training to APHIS.

In other instances, we found that the two agencies had little or limited contact. For example, in one West Coast marine safety office, officials said that they tried for several years to develop a relationship—for example, offering MARPOL V training—with their local APHIS counterparts but were unsuccessful. A senior APHIS official said that some Coast Guard units have asked APHIS personnel to participate in joint boardings and safety inspections, which are beyond what APHIS has agreed to do. In another location on the East Coast, we found that a local APHIS office was mailing its inspection forms with suspected MARPOL V violations to the Coast Guard weeks after the ships had left port. At our suggestion, APHIS began faxing copies of inspection reports to the local Coast Guard units on the same day; this practice will allow the Coast Guard to inspect vessels suspected of violating MARPOL V before the vessels leave port. Coast Guard enforcement personnel told us that they believed that the "personalities" of the local officials involved, coupled with the fact that APHIS has no formal or regulatory responsibility to enforce MARPOL V, are key factors that have contributed to the poor cooperation in some locations.

Efforts to formalize the nature and extent of cooperation between the two agencies have thus far been unsuccessful. For example, beginning in 1993 the Coast Guard sought to develop a memorandum of understanding with APHIS on this issue; however, agreement between the two agencies has still not been achieved. A senior APHIS official told us that he believes that a formal agreement is too "bureaucratic" and is not necessary in this instance. Even without an agreement, the Chief of the Coast Guard's Marine Environmental Protection Division said that the Coast Guard will seek to identify practices found in locations where a productive relationship exists and apply them to those locations where cooperation has been more limited.

Lack of Clear Case Feedback Exists

Clear feedback from Coast Guard hearing officers can provide important information for enforcement personnel in the field on how to develop sound civil penalty cases that are technically correct and include complete evidence. If their cases are well prepared, enforcement personnel can better ensure that cases are not dismissed for technicalities, that proper civil penalties are assessed, and that enforcement time is not wasted. To improve the general quality of cases forwarded for civil penalty proceedings, the Coast Guard's guidance requires hearing officers to notify district managers about the final action taken in each case. This notification should include the rationale the hearing officer used in reaching the decision, according to the hearing officers' program manager. However, district offices are not required to forward the hearing officers' feedback to local units.

Enforcement personnel with whom we talked expressed frustration and confusion about why many MARPOL V cases are dismissed or why civil penalties are reduced. Twenty-two percent of all enforcement cases for the period from October 1, 1991, to December 31, 1994, were closed or dismissed by the Coast Guard without any enforcement action. Also, hearing offices' data indicate that for fiscal years 1992-94, the final penalty assessed by the hearing office averaged less than half the average amount recommended to the hearing office. Enforcement personnel commented that often they receive untimely and/or insufficient feedback or rationale from the hearing officers or district program managers; therefore, the enforcement personnel learn little from the cases that can be applied to improve future submissions. For example, enforcement personnel in several marine safety offices said that it often takes months for their district to pass on to local units information from hearing officers, reducing the ability of unit personnel to learn from the feedback. At another marine safety office, we were told that the unit did not use case file information as a source of feedback because it was so old by the time it was returned. Also, hearing officers do not always provide a rationale for their decisions, according to hearing officers in two different offices.

In cases in which good feedback has been provided, better case preparation has occurred. For example, a hearing officer told us about one marine safety office that had greatly improved the quality of its cases and the corresponding success rate for adjudicating MARPOL V violations. Enforcement personnel at this office told us that the key to the improvement in the quality of its cases stemmed from following the feedback that the office had received from its earlier cases and from the subsequent training that its enforcement personnel received.

The hearing officers' program manager acknowledged that sometimes cases are dismissed or civil penalties reduced because of incomplete case development and technicalities. She indicated that there is a need for good feedback and better case preparation guidance in general; however, because of other higher priorities, no such guidance has been prepared.

Hearing officers with whom we spoke are reluctant to provide feedback on specific cases to the districts or units because of the importance of maintaining their neutrality as an adjudicator and avoiding the appearance of assisting in the prosecution of a particular case. They were amenable, however, to providing more general guidance or training on good case preparation techniques. In fact, some hearing officers said they occasionally visit districts to educate enforcement personnel on this subject, although the frequency of such visits varies.

Marine Safety Information System Is Time-Consuming and Ineffective

The Coast Guard's marine safety information system, the system used to collect and analyze the MARPOL V enforcement data, was frequently cited by Coast Guard officials as burdensome and ineffectual. We previously reported on problems with this system, such as hardware and software problems, untimely and inaccurate information, and user "unfriendliness."[13] The effect of these problems on enforcing MARPOL is threefold. First, time spent trying to input data (as much as 10 hours for

---

[13]Coast Guard: Progress in the Marine Safety Network, but Many Uncertainties Remain (GAO/RCED-92-206, Aug. 28, 1992).

each violation) takes time away from inspecting ships. Second, program managers do not have access to data when they need them in order to monitor or evaluate the performance of marine safety offices. Collecting needed data by other means can be a laborious process, resulting in the ineffective use of staff at the unit level. For example, from March 1992 until October 1994, the Coast Guard—in an effort to collect accurate data and provide feedback to the field—tasked each marine safety office to manually collect enforcement data separately from the system. These data were reported monthly to program managers in Coast Guard headquarters, who otherwise would have had to wait 4 to 6 months for the system to report the same information. Third, the system does not include complete data on enforcement cases generated by Coast Guard personnel outside of marine safety offices, such as those cases recorded by small boat station personnel. In our view, this situation makes coordination among various Coast Guard units more difficult to achieve in enforcing MARPOL V.

The Coast Guard is now completing some improvements to the system that it hopes will overcome the obstacles discussed above. According to the Chief of the Coast Guard's Marine Environmental Protection Division, improving the MARPOL component of the data system has been a high priority in the Coast Guard and is expected to reduce input time and speed data collection for MARPOL violations. In addition, a contract was recently let to begin the development of the Coast Guard's next management information system, according to Coast Guard headquarters officials. However, this new system will not be in operation for at least 2 years.

Utilization of MARPOL Billets Is Uncertain

For fiscal year 1991, the Senate Committee on Appropriations provided for 100 positions for pollution prevention activities. The Coast Guard designated 85 of these positions as "MARPOL investigator" or "coastal pollution enforcement" positions and allocated the remaining 15 positions as a support and training allowance. Coast Guard documents indicate that all but one of these positions were filled during 1991 and 1992.

According to Coast Guard officials in headquarters and the field, MARPOL enforcement efforts are better spread among a number of personnel in each marine safety office rather than limited to the 85 designated enforcement personnel. As a result, the designated MARPOL personnel do not spend their time exclusively on MARPOL activities. We found that some spend less than half their time on MARPOL activities, while other personnel also perform MARPOL-related duties. However, we were unable to determine how much time, in the aggregate, the Coast Guard spends on

MARPOL-related activities because its personnel do not regularly record their MARPOL-related activities. For example, MARPOL-related time charges actually reported by the marine safety information system for the 1-year period from July 1, 1993, to June 30, 1994, totaled just less than 12,500 hours (or a little over the work time of seven full-time equivalent positions).[14] However, according to Coast Guard officials familiar with the system, few personnel strictly account for MARPOL time charges because such accounting has not been required and is viewed by personnel as burdensome.

The Coast Guard believes a better estimate of the time devoted to MARPOL each year, including all enforcement and education activities, is about that of 61 to 66 full-time equivalent staff. However, the reliability of this estimate is suspect because it is based on an extrapolation of the time charges of just one marine safety office. There is no assurance that the situation at this office is representative of MARPOL enforcement activities at marine safety offices as a whole, particularly since we noted considerable differences in the level of MARPOL V enforcement activities among the offices we visited.

Education Has Become an Important Part of the Coast Guard's MARPOL Strategy

The Coast Guard has determined that enforcement alone will not achieve compliance with MARPOL V, and enforcement for some sectors of the marine community is not viable. Therefore, the Coast Guard has embarked on an education and outreach effort to improve compliance. Since the early 1990s, the Coast Guard has conducted MARPOL education. Initially, education was focused on informing the maritime industry about the new MARPOL regulations as an extension of the Coast Guard's enforcement activities—for example, handing out pamphlets and stickers to commercial shippers and port facility managers. The emphasis has now expanded to educate recreational boaters and the commercial fishing industry about maritime pollution. Because of the high numbers and dispersion of recreational boats and fishing vessels, enforcement through inspections, patrols, or similar means is nearly impossible.[15] Education appears to be a reasonable strategy for this group and one supported by the Center for Marine Conservation.[16]

---

[14]The Coast Guard assumes that one annual full-time equivalent position represents 212 8-hour days, 1,696 hours.

[15]The Center for Marine Conservation estimates that there are 46 million recreational boaters in the United States, while the Coast Guard reported that almost 45,000 commercial fishing vessels were registered in the United States in fiscal year 1993.

[16]The Center for Marine Conservation, established in 1972, is a nonprofit public interest group dedicated to protecting marine wildlife and conserving coastal and ocean resources.

Education and Outreach Funded by a Department of Defense Grant	In March 1994, the Coast Guard's existing education and outreach efforts were increased through a $1.28 million grant from the Department of Defense's Civil Military Cooperation Action Program to begin a pilot program. The pilot, known as the SeaPartners Campaign, received another grant of $1.7 million for fiscal year 1995. The Coast Guard has applied for grant money again for fiscal year 1996, the last year that the pilot is eligible under this grant program. After 1996, the Coast Guard plans to fund the campaign internally.

During 1994, Seapartners Generated Considerable, Although Somewhat Unfocused, Activity

The Coast Guard initiated the SeaPartners Campaign with a wide range of activities. To design the campaign, the Coast Guard worked with the Center for Marine Conservation as well as many federal, state, and local agencies. In June 1994, Coast Guard headquarters sponsored training for active-duty personnel and reservists to help them undertake public outreach and education at their home units.[17] Following the training, the participants returned to their home units and began educating a wide range of audiences, from other Coast Guard personnel to grade school children, on marine pollution. The Coast Guard estimates that by September 1994, the campaign had reached about 175,000 people through 1,180 separate activities in various parts of the country.

During our visits to marine safety offices, we noted considerable support and enthusiasm for the SeaPartners program among Coast Guard personnel. The offices were supporting a wide variety of educational activities, and personnel said that they were receiving positive feedback from the public. Just how the program is contributing to MARPOL V enforcement is unknown, however, because no good measure of this has been developed.

In 1994, the Coast Guard commissioned an outside evaluation of SeaPartners. The evaluation determined that while the campaign generated considerable activity, its mission needed to be clarified and its activities needed to be better targeted.[18] While concluding that the pilot had great potential to make substantial contributions to protecting the marine environment, the report noted that SeaPartners was so broadly defined that there were "misperceptions, confusion, and a lack of common understanding about the program's goals, objectives, and mission and appropriate ways to achieve the program's intended outcome." The report

---

[17]In 1994, the pilot program was staffed by 259 reservists and 49 active duty personnel.

[18]A.T. Kearney, Inc., Results of the SEA-KEEPERS Campaign Pilot Months (April Through September 1994), Final Report, November 1994 (Alexandria, Va.).

made 31 recommendations on ways to strengthen public outreach. The Coast Guard agreed with the report's recommendations and has revised its strategy for SeaPartners in fiscal year 1995. The new strategy clarifies SeaPartners' mission, targets activities toward more traditional port community audiences, and develops ways to measure the campaign's effects.

Conclusions

The Coast Guard has made progress in its enforcement of MARPOL V through heightened awareness at the unit level and the development of a broader-based education and outreach program. It still faces a number of formidable obstacles to further enhance enforcement in this area, however. We believe that improving the ability of its personnel to identify violations and better substantiate them in their enforcement actions is critical to achieving this end. Doing so would involve improving procedures for vessel inspections, establishing a better working relationship with APHIS, and providing useful and timely feedback to units. It is also important that the Coast Guard continue its efforts to improve its education and outreach program for MARPOL V and its management information system used to monitor the performance of field units in achieving MARPOL V enforcement.

Recommendations

We recommend that the Secretary of Transportation direct the Commandant of the U.S. Coast Guard to do the following:

- Develop and put into force a standardized MARPOL V inspection checklist for use by its enforcement personnel. Doing so will improve the Coast Guard's ability to identify and properly document violations.
- Develop procedures to ensure that case feedback from hearing officers, including the rationale for decisions made, is provided to districts and forwarded to local units in a timely manner.
- Explore with the Administrator of APHIS areas of mutual interest and ways to improve cooperation between the U.S. Coast Guard and APHIS on enforcing MARPOL V.

Agency Comments

We provided copies of a draft of this report to the Coast Guard and the Animal and Plant Health Inspection Service, U.S. Department of Agriculture, for their comments. We discussed the information in the draft report with Coast Guard officials, including the Chief of the Marine Environment and Protection Division. We also discussed the draft report with the Assistant to the Deputy Administrator, Plant Protection and Quarantine Service, Animal and Plant Health Inspection Service. These officials agreed with the facts as presented, but the Coast Guard contended that the content and tone of the draft did not give the Coast Guard adequate credit for the positive results that it has achieved and the efforts that it has made to improve the program. We have modified the final report where appropriate to recognize improvements to the program. The Coast Guard agreed with our recommendations for a standardized checklist and procedures to ensure case feedback from hearing officers. It disagreed with our proposed recommendation that the Secretaries of Transportation and Agriculture should intercede, if necessary, to ensure cooperation between the Coast Guard and APHIS. We agree that cooperation could be sought at a lower level and have revised the recommendation to encourage the Commandant of the Coast Guard and the Administrator of APHIS to explore ways to improve their cooperation.

We conducted our work between June 1994 and April 1995 in accordance with generally accepted government auditing standards. During that time, we contacted Coast Guard field and headquarters offices, met with interested outside parties, and analyzed the Coast Guard's violation data. Details of our scope and methodology are provided in appendix II.

As agreed, unless you publicly announce its contents earlier, we plan no further distribution of the report until 7 days from the date of this letter. At that time, we will send copies to the Secretary of Transportation; the Commandant, U.S. Coast Guard; the Secretary of Agriculture; the Administrator of the Animal and Plant Health Inspection Service, U.S. Department of Agriculture; the Director, Office of Management and Budget; and other interested parties. We will make copies available to others on request.

Please call me at (202) 512-2834 if you have questions. Major contributors to this report are listed in appendix III.

Kenneth M. Mead
Director, Transportation Issues

Contents

Abbreviations

APHIS	Animal and Plant Health Inspection Service
COTP/MIO	Captain of the Port/Marine Inspection Office
GAO	General Accounting Office
MSO	Marine Safety Office
MARPOL V	International Convention for the Prevention of Pollution From Ships, Annex V

Analysis of MARPOL V Violations and Enforcement Results

Our analysis of MARPOL V enforcement data is drawn from two data sets. The first are enforcement data from cases initiated by marine safety offices (MSO). The second set are data for only those cases processed by hearing offices for civil penalty determination, but from all sources, including law enforcement and boating safety personnel.

Marine Safety Office Enforcement Data

MSOS' MARPOL V enforcement data span the period from October 1, 1991, to December 31, 1994 (fiscal years 1992, 1993, 1994 and the first quarter of 1995). A total of 725 enforcement cases were reported during this period. The sections below discuss the status of these cases as of February 15, 1995.

Enforcement Trends Since October 1, 1991

The number of enforcement cases initiated by MSOS have generally followed an upward trend (see fig. I.1). The main exception was in the third and fourth quarter of 1993, when the number of cases initiated fell before starting back up in 1994.

Figure I.1: MARPOL V Violations by Quarter

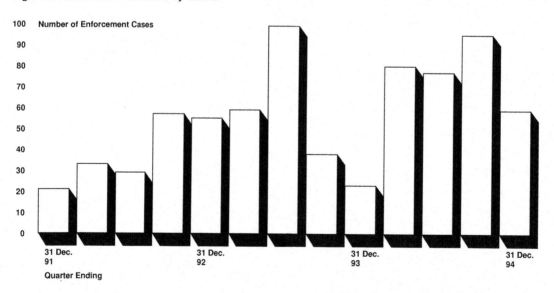

Note: Cases reported from Oct. 1, 1991, through Dec. 31, 1994.

Disposition and Status of Enforcement Cases

Final action has been taken on 422 of the 725 enforcement cases
(58 percent), while 303 remain in process. The greatest portion of
completed cases (157 cases) were administratively closed by the MSO or
district offices, or dismissed by the hearing office for insufficient evidence
(see fig. I.2). Another 129 cases were referred to the responsible party's
flag state for action because U.S. jurisdiction could not be proven or was
not applied. In only 9 out of the 129 referrals did the flag state ultimately
fine the responsible party. A State Department official told us that flag
state referrals are typically marginal cases that are short on evidence.
Another 67 enforcement cases were closed with a warning letter to the
responsible party, while 69 cases resulted in a penalty.

Figure I.2: Disposition and Status of MARPOL V Enforcement Cases

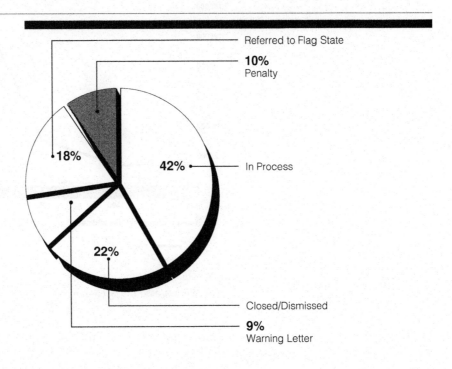

Note: Cases reported from Oct. 1, 1991, through Dec. 31, 1994.

Trends in Penalty Amounts

An analysis of the 69 enforcement cases that have thus far resulted in a penalty shows that the average has generally risen from $4,250 in 1989 to $8,750 in 1994 (see fig. I.3).[19] The increasing number of enforcement cases from 1989 to 1992 caused the total amount of penalties to increase. The drop in total penalties after 1992, shown in figure I.3, reflects the fact that a high percentage of cases initiated in 1993 and 1994 are still in process.

Figure I.3: Total and Average Penalties Assessed

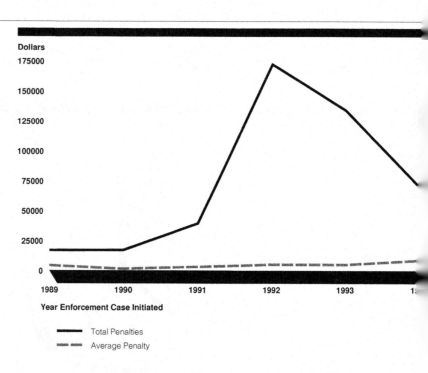

Dollars

Year Enforcement Case Initiated

—— Total Penalties
▬ ▬ Average Penalty

Note: Penalties assessed for cases reported from Jan. 1, 1989, through Dec. 31, 1994.

Distribution of Enforcement Cases Among District Offices

Enforcement cases are not distributed evenly among district offices, as figure I.4 indicates. District 8, which includes MSOs bordering the Gulf of Mexico, has accounted for more than one-fourth of all cases. Districts 7 (Southeastern U.S. and Puerto Rico) and 14 (Hawaii and Guam) together have accounted for over 30 percent. Districts on the East (1 and 5) and

---

[19]While outside of the detailed MSO data set used elsewhere, civil penalty and enforcement case tota for 1989 through 1991 were taken from Coast Guard documents. Penalty amounts include one violat that resulted in a criminal penalty assessment imposed by the Department of Justice.

West Coasts (11 and 13) have accounted for comparatively fewer, while inland districts (2 and 9) have accounted for the fewest number of cases.

Figure I.4: MARPOL V Enforcement Cases by District Office

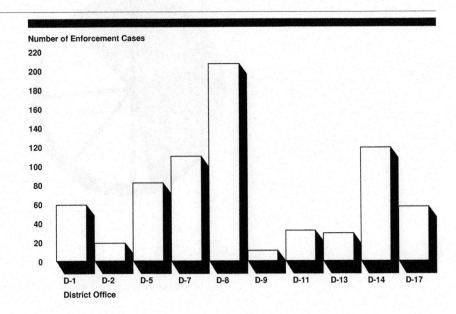

Note: Cases by district office from Oct. 1, 1991, through Dec. 31, 1994.

Types of Violations

Most of the enforcement cases, as shown in figure I.5, were based on violations of regulations prohibiting the discharge of plastic or garbage. Less serious infractions, such as failure to post a garbage sign or maintain a waste management plan, have been cited less frequently.

**Figure I.5: MARPOL V Enforcement
Cases by Type of Violation**

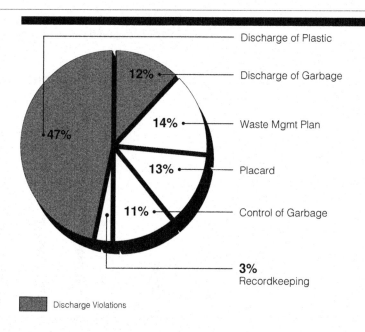

Discharge of Plastic

Discharge of Garbage

12%

Waste Mgmt Plan

14%

47%

Placard

13%

Control of Garbage

11%

3%
Recordkeeping

Discharge Violations

Note: Violations from Oct. 1, 1991, through Dec. 31, 1994.

Civil penalties were assessed more often for cases where garbage or
plastic was discharged. Of the 69 enforcement cases that resulted in a
penalty, 84 percent (58 violations) were discharge cases. These 58
discharge violations also accounted for 98 percent of the total penalty
dollars assessed.

Flag State Enforcement Cases

A majority of the enforcement cases involved ships licensed (or "flagged"
in other countries, although as figure I.6 also shows, 4 out of 10 cases wer
for U.S.-licensed vessels. The Coast Guard conducts more inspections of
U.S. ships than foreign ships—38,303 boardings of U.S. ships versus 16,02
boardings of foreign ships in fiscal year 1993. Vessels flagged by Panama,
Liberia, and the Bahamas, often referred to as flags of convenience
because the owners are not citizens of the flag state, accounted for the
highest percentages of foreign-flag enforcement cases.

Figure I.6: MARPOL V Enforcement Cases by Flag State

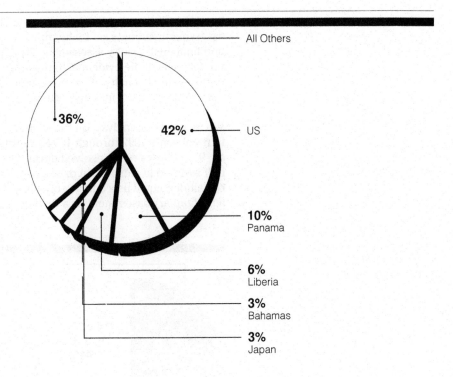

Note: Enforcement cases by flag state from Oct. 1, 1991, through Dec. 31, 1994.

Hearing Offices' Data on Disposition of Cases

The Coast Guard's Division of Maritime and International Law maintains its own set of MARPOL V enforcement data drawn from the marine safety information system. The division provided us with data covering all cases submitted to the Coast Guard's three hearing offices in fiscal years 1992 through 1994. Legal staff use these data to monitor hearing offices' disposition of civil penalty cases. Unlike the MSOs' data, which are organized by enforcement case, these data are organized by citation charge, that is, the section of the regulation found to be in noncompliance. Some enforcement cases may involve more than one charge. For each charge, the data include the civil penalty amounts recommended to the hearing office by the district program managers, preliminary civil penalty assessment amounts set by hearing officers prior to a civil penalty hearing and final civil penalty assessment amounts. Hearing officers may decide, on the basis of the evidence, to dismiss a charge, issue a warning letter, or impose a final penalty. In some instances, the party may decide to pay the preliminary penalty amount rather than going through the hearing process.

We focused our analysis on those charges that hearing officers had closed in fiscal years 1992 through 1994, omitting any that were still in process. In all, 928 charges were resolved during the 3-year period. Of these, just over half resulted in a dismissal or warning letter (see fig. I.7). Of the remainder, equal percentages of charges (24 percent) were settled through a preliminary assessment or a final penalty assessment.

Figure I.7: Hearing Offices' Final Dispositions of MARPOL V Enforcement Cases

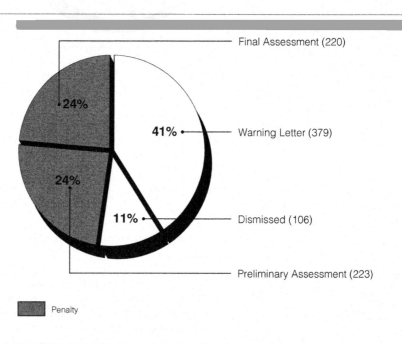

Penalty

Note: Dispositions from Oct. 1, 1991, through Sept. 30, 1994.

Hearing Offices' Civil Penalty Assessments

Total recommended and preliminary civil penalty amounts increased substantially during fiscal years 1992-94 (see fig. I.8). In fiscal year 1994, for example, units recommended $753,746 in total civil penalties, a

73 percent increase over the previous year. By comparison, the final civil
penalties assessed have not increased as dramatically—indeed, totals
declined somewhat for fiscal year 1994.

Figure I.8: Total Civil Penalty Amounts

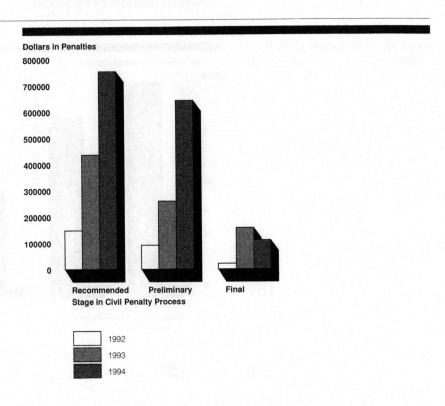

Note: Penalty amounts from Oct. 1, 1991, through Sept. 30, 1994.

Examining the average civil penalty amounts for just the charges in which
a penalty was imposed (excluding charges resulting in dismissal or a
warning letter) also shows a substantial decline between recommended
and final civil penalty amounts for fiscal years 1992-94 (see fig. I.9). For the
3-year period, the average final civil penalty was more than 50 percent less
than the average penalty recommended to the hearing office. Hearing
officers said that units establish civil penalty amounts strictly based on
guidance from headquarters and without knowing the violator's side of the

story. The hearing officers, after reviewing rebuttals and other information
from the vessel operator or owner, frequently reduce a civil penalty based
on a much broader knowledge base than unit personnel have when they
initially recommend a civil penalty.

Figure I.9: Average Civil Penalty Per Charge

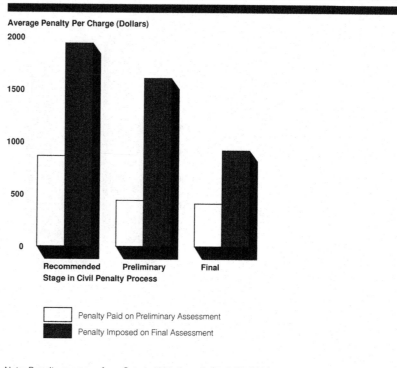

Average Penalty Per Charge (Dollars)

Stage in Civil Penalty Process

☐ Penalty Paid on Preliminary Assessment

■ Penalty Imposed on Final Assessment

Note: Penalty averages from Oct. 1, 1991, through Sept. 30, 1994.

Scope and Methodology

To evaluate the Coast Guard's efforts to enforce MARPOL V, we conducted work at Coast Guard headquarters and at numerous field locations. At Coast Guard headquarters in Washington, D.C., we interviewed and obtained documents from program managers in the Office of Marine Safety, Security, and Environmental Protection, the office responsible for implementing the Coast Guard's MARPOL V program. We also met with Coast Guard officials in the Office of Chief Counsel, the Office of Navigation Safety and Waterway Services, and the Office of Law Enforcement and Defense Operations, which also are charged with enforcement responsibility.

In the field, we visited 4 of the Coast Guard's 10 district offices to understand their role in enforcement and all three of the Coast Guard's hearing offices (Atlantic North, Atlantic South, and Pacific Area) to discuss the civil penalty process. We also visited 9 of the Coast Guard's 47 MSOs, which are responsible for enforcing MARPOL V in U.S. ports. The MSOs we visited were judgmentally selected on the basis of MARPOL V case activity (high and low activity) and to achieve a broad geographical representation among offices on the East, West, and Gulf Coasts. At the MSOs, we participated in vessel inspections in addition to meeting with enforcement personnel. Table II.1 provides a list of the MSO and district offices visited as part of our review.

Table II.1: Marine Safety Offices and District Offices Visited as Part of This Review

District office	Marine safety office
District 1 (Boston)	MSO Boston
	COTP/MIO[a] New York
	MSO Portland, Maine
District 8 (New Orleans)	MSO New Orleans
	MSO Corpus Christi
District 11 (Los Angeles/Long Beach)	MSO San Francisco
	MSO Los Angeles/Long Beach
District 13 (Seattle)	MSO Puget Sound
	MSO Portland, Oregon

[a]Captain of the Port/Marine Inspection Office.

A significant part of our evaluation consisted of analyzing the Coast Guard's enforcement case data. Our analysis was based largely on data from the Coast Guard's marine safety information system on MARPOL V enforcement cases initiated by MSOs for the period from October 1, 1991, through December 31, 1994. These data included the date, MSO, ship name, type of vessel, licensing country, type(s) of violation(s), current status and if applicable, penalty amount for each violation case. Another set of MARPOL V data came from the Office of Chief Counsel and included only those enforcement cases that reached the hearing office for civil penalty determination in fiscal years 1992 through 1994. While excluding the significant number of cases that were closed or referred elsewhere before reaching the hearing office, it included cases reported by law enforcement and boating safety personnel. We did not audit the accuracy of any of the Coast Guard's enforcement data, although we did attempt to eliminate duplicate entries and erroneous entries. Appendix I discusses the analysis of each of these sets of data.

In addition to our work at the Coast Guard, we met with officials from other federal agencies and outside entities familiar with MARPOL V. We interviewed officials from the Department of Agriculture's Animal and Plant Health Inspection Service, the Environmental Protection Agency, the Center for Marine Conservation, and the National Marine Board. We also reviewed reports on the MARPOL V program by the Department of Transportation's Inspector General, outside consultants, and congressional committees.

To assess the Coast Guard's utilization of MARPOL personnel resources, we determined if the Coast Guard had assigned personnel to these dedicated positions and, to the extent possible, the range of their duties and responsibilities. We examined the Coast Guard's records for indications of the amount of time spent on MARPOL-related activities.

To describe the Coast Guard's educational and outreach efforts pertaining to MARPOL V, we met with Coast Guard officials in headquarters and in the field. We identified the Coast Guard's strategy for this effort and how it was being implemented. At the nine MSOs we visited, we reviewed the specific actions being taken in their educational outreach. We also discussed the Coast Guard's efforts with the Center for Marine Conservation, which has been active in this area for many years. We reviewed an outside consultant's report on the education program, discussed its findings and recommendations with responsible Coast Guard officials, and ascertained what the Coast Guard was doing in response.

RESOURCES, COMMUNITY, AND ECONOMIC DEVELOPMENT
DIVISION

Paul Aussendorf
Gerald Dillingham
Steve Gazda
Dawn Hoff
Stan Stenersen
Charles Sylvis
Randy Williamson

Ordering Information

The first copy of each GAO report and testimony is free.
Additional copies are $2 each. Orders should be sent to the
following address, accompanied by a check or money order
made out to the Superintendent of Documents, when
necessary. Orders for 100 or more copies to be mailed to a
single address are discounted 25 percent.

Orders by mail:

U.S. General Accounting Office
P.O. Box 6015
Gaithersburg, MD 20884-6015

or visit:

Room 1100
700 4th St. NW (corner of 4th and G Sts. NW)
U.S. General Accounting Office
Washington, DC

Orders may also be placed by calling (202) 512-6000
or by using fax number (301) 258-4066, or TDD (301) 413-0006.

Each day, GAO issues a list of newly available reports and
testimony. To receive facsimile copies of the daily list or any
list from the past 30 days, please call (301) 258-4097 using a
touchtone phone. A recorded menu will provide information on
how to obtain these lists.

United States
General Accounting Office
Washington, D.C. 20548-0001

Official Business
Penalty for Private Use $300

Address Correction Requested

CPSIA information can be obtained at www.ICGtesting.com
Printed in the USA
BVOW09s2145210416

445186BV00008B/72/P